CROCODILE MONITOR VS. SOUTHERN CASSOWARY

BY NATHAN SOMMER

BELLWETHER MEDIA • MINNEAPOLIS, MN

™

Torque brims with excitement
perfect for thrill-seekers of all kinds.
Discover daring survival skills, explore
uncharted worlds, and marvel at mighty
engines and extreme sports. In *Torque* books,
anything can happen. Are you ready?

This edition first published in 2024 by Bellwether Media, Inc.

No part of this publication may be reproduced in whole or in part without written
permission of the publisher. For information regarding permission, write to
Bellwether Media, Inc., Attention: Permissions Department,
6012 Blue Circle Drive, Minnetonka, MN 55343.

Library of Congress Cataloging-in-Publication Data

LC record for Crocodile Monitor vs. Southern Cassowary available at:
https://lccn.loc.gov/2023000643

Editor: Kieran Downs   Designer: Josh Brink

Printed in the United States of America, North Mankato, MN.

TABLE OF CONTENTS

THE COMPETITORS 4

SECRET WEAPONS...................10

ATTACK MOVES......................16

READY, FIGHT! 20

GLOSSARY............................ 22

TO LEARN MORE 23

INDEX 24

THE COMPETITORS

The **rain forests** of Southeast Asia are home to some tough animals. Crocodile monitors are **apex predators**. These giant **reptiles** face little competition for food.

Southern cassowaries are dangerous animals, too. These speedy, giant birds pack a deadly kick. Who wins when these two animals face off?

CROCODILE MONITOR PROFILE

LENGTH
UP TO 16.4 FEET
(5 METERS)

WEIGHT
UP TO 198 POUNDS
(90 KILOGRAMS)

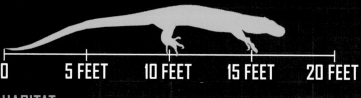

0   5 FEET   10 FEET   15 FEET   20 FEET

HABITAT

RAIN FORESTS

SWAMPS

CROCODILE MONITOR RANGE

RANGE

Crocodile monitors are some of the world's longest lizards. They grow up to 16.4 feet (5 meters) long. They weigh up to 198 pounds (90 kilograms).

These lizards have blackish-green bodies with yellow spots and long tails. They spend most of their time in the trees of Southeast Asia's rain forests and swamps.

ALL IN A NAME

Crocodile monitors were named because their teeth are very similar to crocodile teeth.

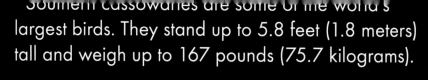

Southern cassowaries are some of the world's largest birds. They stand up to 5.8 feet (1.8 meters) tall and weigh up to 167 pounds (75.7 kilograms).

These flightless birds have blue heads with two red **wattles**. They also have helmet-like structures called **casques**. They live in the rain forests and swamps of Indonesia, Papua New Guinea, and northeastern Australia.

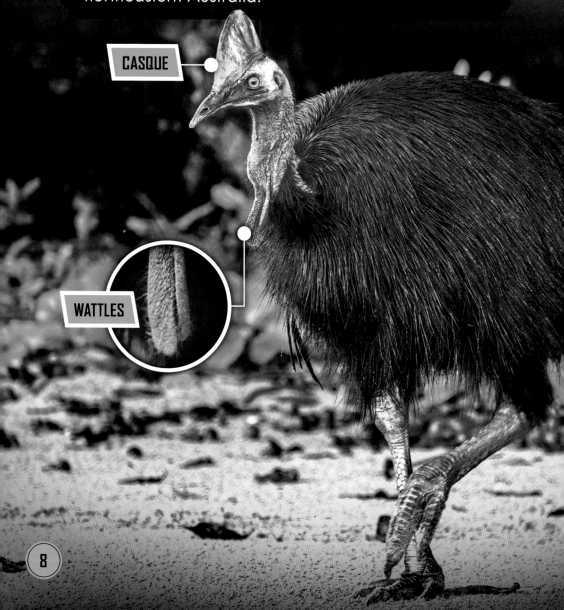

CASQUE

WATTLES

SOUTHERN CASSOWARY PROFILE

LENGTH
UP TO 5.8 FEET
(1.8 METERS)

WEIGHT
UP TO 167 POUNDS
(75.7 KILOGRAMS)

- 6 FEET
- 5 FEET
- 4 FEET
- 3 FEET
- 2 FEET
- 1 FOOT
- 0

HABITAT

RAIN FORESTS

SWAMPS

SOUTHERN CASSOWARY RANGE

 RANGE

SECRET WEAPONS

Crocodile monitors smell with their long, forked tongues. Their tongues help them easily track down **prey**. The lizards are very hard to hide from!

Southern cassowaries have strong legs. They help the birds jump up to 7 feet (2.1 meters) high. They also use their legs to deliver powerful kicks to enemies.

DANGER

Southern cassowaries are often considered the world's most dangerous birds!

CROCODILE MONITOR TAIL
OVER 8 FEET (2.4 METERS)

| 0 | 2 FEET | 4 FEET | 6 FEET | 8 FEET | 10 FEET |

AVERAGE COUCH
7 FEET (2.1 METERS)

| 0 | 2 FEET | 4 FEET | 6 FEET | 8 FEET | 10 FEET |

Crocodile monitors have long tails. These grow to be more than 8 feet (2.4 meters) long. They are used as a whip against enemies. Their tails also help them balance while climbing trees.

Southern cassowaries have super speed. They can run up to 31 miles (50 kilometers) per hour. The birds easily escape most enemies.

FORKED TONGUES

LONG TAILS

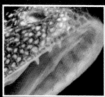

SHARP, SERRATED TEETH

Sharp, **serrated** teeth line the mouths of crocodile monitors. The lizards use these to slice and tear into prey. The teeth also hold prey in place as the lizards climb trees.

SECRET WEAPO

POWERFUL LEGS

SPEED

SHARP CL.

SOUTHE
CASSOWAR

UP TO 5
(12.7 CENT

Southern cassowaries have sharp claws on e
toe. The middle claw is the longest. It can be u
5 inches (12.7 centimeters) long. They easily

ATTACK MOVES

Crocodile monitors are not afraid to fight. The lizards roll their tails up when threatened. This warns enemies to stay away. They whip their powerful tails at attackers who do not back down!

Southern cassowaries often fight when threatened. They stretch their feathers and stand taller to appear larger. They charge forward at enemies who do not back off!

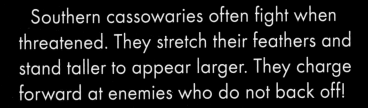

CASSOWARY CALLS

Cassowaries talk to each other using low, booming calls. The calls are so low that humans cannot always hear them.

Crocodile monitors **stalk** their prey.
They catch small prey in their mouths.
Then, they carry their food up a tree to eat.

CROCODILE MONITOR DIET

Crocodile monitors feed mostly on
mice and small birds. They also eat
fish and the eggs of other animals.

Southern cassowaries charge in fights. They jump and kick at enemies. Then, they stomp once attackers are on the ground. The birds also attack with their beaks.

READY, FIGHT!

A large crocodile monitor stalks a southern cassowary. The giant bird could provide a great feast! The monitor whips its tail. It knocks the cassowary down.

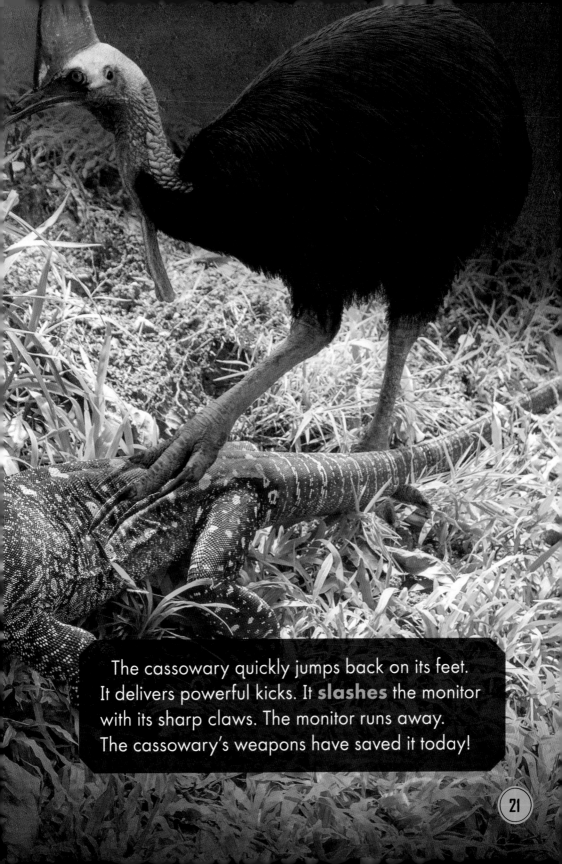

The cassowary quickly jumps back on its feet. It delivers powerful kicks. It **slashes** the monitor with its sharp claws. The monitor runs away. The cassowary's weapons have saved it today!

GLOSSARY

apex predators—animals at the top of the food chain that are not preyed upon by other animals

casques—helmet-like structures on the heads of cassowaries

prey—animals that are hunted by other animals for food

rain forests—thick, green forests that receive a lot of rain

reptiles—cold-blooded animals that have backbones and lay eggs

serrated—having a blade like that of a saw

slashes—cuts with a sharp object

stalk—to follow closely and quietly

wattles—sagging pieces of skin at the bottom of the chin

TO LEARN MORE

AT THE LIBRARY

Sommer, Nathan. *Komodo Dragon vs. Orangutan*. Minneapolis, Minn.: Bellwether Media, 2021.

Sommer, Nathan. *Ostrich vs. Cheetah*. Minneapolis, Minn.: Bellwether Media, 2023.

Vonder Brink, Tracy. *Reptiles*. New York, N.Y.: Crabtree Publishing, 2023.

ON THE WEB

FACTSURFER

Factsurfer.com gives you a safe, fun way to find more information.

1. Go to www.factsurfer.com

2. Enter "crocodile monitor vs. southern cassowary" into the search box and click 🔍.

3. Select your book cover to see a list of related content.

INDEX

apex predators, 4

attackers, 16, 19

Australia, 8

beaks, 19

birds, 5, 8, 11, 13, 18, 19, 20

calls, 17

casques, 8

claws, 15, 21

color, 7, 8

diet, 18

enemies, 11, 12, 13, 15, 16, 17, 19

feathers, 17

fight, 16, 17, 19

habitat, 4, 6, 7, 8, 9

Indonesia, 8

kicks, 5, 11, 19, 21

legs, 11

mouths, 14, 18

name, 7

Papua New Guinea, 8

prey, 10, 14, 18

range, 4, 6, 7, 8, 9

reptiles, 4

size, 4, 5, 6, 7, 8, 9, 12, 15, 17, 20

Southeast Asia, 4, 7

speed, 5, 13

stalk, 18, 20

tails, 7, 12, 16, 20

teeth, 7, 14

tongues, 10

trees, 7, 12, 14, 18

wattles, 8

weapons, 14, 15, 21

The images in this book are reproduced through the courtesy of: reptiles4all, front cover (crocodile monitor, crocodile monitor neck), p. 14 (crocodile monitor; sharp, serrated teeth); Jenylovely, front cover (southern cassowary); Danny Ye, pp. 2-3, 12, 14 (forked tongues, long tails), 18, 20-21, 22-23, 24; Kevin Schafer, pp. 3, 21, 23; Fabrice Bettex Photography/ Alamy, p. 4; Ezzolo, p. 5; slowmotiongli, pp. 6-7; Ian Beattie/ Alamy, pp. 8-9; Rob D the Baker, p. 9 (wattles); Robert Franklin Photography, p. 10; wildestanimal/ Getty, p. 11; S A B R I N A B A L I/ wiki commons, p. 15 (powerful legs); ozflash, p. 15 (speed); Fazwick, p. 15 (sharp claws); Paula Petrucci, p. 15; Mikhail Blajenov, p. 16; icosha, p. 17; Mark Newman/ Getty, p. 19.